MW00412641

In honor of the wonderful souls that must be strong and accepting of themselves by life circumstances beyond their control, I have been honored to gift a portion of this book's proceeds to the National Alopecia Areata Foundation. (www.naaf.org)

#BaldisBeautiful #LoveYourBeauty

Sam,
To the beautiful badass I love so much! ♡ Hallee Hope
I love you beautiful

Table of Contents:

Forward

Taking the time to read this book shows a seeking to gain a new perspective, to see the world with new understanding. Often times there are lessons that authors, teachers and friends intend to illustrate. We share our naked words openly with the world in hopes that some portion of our words our reach reader's hearts. Because we are driven by a natural human desire to share what we have learned from experiences, specific messages are shared with those we love. I thank you for taking the time to let me share my heart and my tough life lessons with you.

These words do not come from a textbook, a certification, or ancient tablets. They are simply insights gained from overcoming obstacles, seeing the positive in every challenge and the drive to shorten the learning curve for all of us. There will be grammatical errors and type-os as I am human, and I am okay with that. *(Especially because I am giving proceeds to a charity organization.)*

When we open up ourselves to new insights, we gain the most insights. By collaborating and sharing our own experiences and insights with each other we actually are able to expand our understanding and see things from different perspectives which allow us to widen our own personal view. Even if it's not the original anticipated lesson, I hope that you will get so much more out of reading these few words that I have to share with you today.

In the world of understanding ourselves, self-love is a term widely used as a blanket statement of why we aren't getting all we desire in life, or how we can proactively create better things in life. While taking care of ourselves and thinking highly of ourselves is very important, it seems the term has taken us to a dark level of destruction rather than empowerment as it has suggested so often in the past.

You may or may not feel your self-love levels are currently exactly where you would like them to be, healthy. Perhaps, there are deeper levels of understanding yet to be discovered within yourself. You could even be one of the lucky few that is a master at self-love! I welcome your curiosity as I unfold what I have discovered about how we love ourselves and how we can also simply love life.

Introduction

The Death of the Self Love Excuse

Some of the best journeys start with a death. Death offers the opportunity to create a new experience, new understanding and new perspectives. If you feel so inspired, you are welcome to stop reading to go cut some roses off the neighbors bush and break out the cheesy funeral potatoes to comfort you while you read, because the *self-love excuse* needs to DIE.

This is not your normal *"self improvement to change how you're thinking and increase spiritual understanding"* book. Nor is this an attack on those who choose to focus increasing and understanding deeper self-love, or even belittling those who choose to base their whole lives around learning how to teach us how to love ourselves. *(I still claim to be one of them myself.)*

This is a book about how to rethink how we love ourselves and examine if we have been damaging ourselves and our relationships in the name of SELF-LOVE. This excuse is no longer something that we need to focus our attention on, rather we can find true love for ourselves and others from a more authentic and loving space than what has been previously presented. *(And that's the extent of my politically correctness, blame the fairness statements on being a middle child.)*

Of course self-love is important. However, is self-love the answer to why we don't allow ourselves to make enough money, why we don't allow ourselves to have the lovely life we feel we desire? Is the lack of self-love why we feel we deserve less, why we self-sabotage, why we second-guess ourselves, or why we are insecure? The list of ways our lives are impacted by a lack of self-love is endless. I would be the first to raise my hand and admit that I found it all too easy to blame self-love for all of my personal shortcomings.

It comes so naturally when things are not going our way for us to simply say, "I must not be enough." or to question what we must fix to receive our desires. We may even resolve that we are broken, or less than and need to settle, only to have outside influences tell us that our problem isn't really the fact that *we* aren't in enough, it's that we don't "love ourselves enough."

This reasoning comes from the belief that someone who loves themselves enough would never settle for second a second rate relationship. If someone truly "loved themselves enough" they would never take on more than they can chew, would never say, "Yes!" when really, they should've said, "No." Someone who loves themselves enough would always know their worth and would walk around feeling a sense of desire and allow themselves to receive all the good things in life.

A person that loves themselves enough would show up in the world fully present, forgetting all about themselves and being able to focus on other people. They would know their worth and demand respect from everyone interacting with them, they could even be viewed as one who feels entitled to better things than what they have with less work than they have put into it. (*Because they obviously deserve all the best.*)

Someone loving themselves, would never be intimate with somebody whom they weren't fully committed to in a relationship, or didn't 100% show up as the person of their dreams. That would be settling for less, and if they really love themselves they would never settle for less. Never settle for mediocre job or doing something to please someone else instead of pleasing themselves, even though they do get pleasure from pleasing other people *(but of course that's not true self-love, that's because you "don't love yourself enough and you need external validation.")*

I may sound opinionated and harsh, however some part of this may speak to some pain, some lack of love within you. I'm there with you, we learn the most through our own experiences and witnessing others struggles and triumphs.

It is time we allowed ourselves to be who we are, to truly love who we are and no longer use the self-love excuse as a crutch to keep us from feeling completely happy with the person we are, the relationships we cultivate and the successes we invite into our lives.

As part of my personal journey, I have spent years seeking self-love. I grew up in a home that wasn't the most nurturing environment for a woman to feel independent, strong, emotionally stable, or able to handle her emotions. I had a hot temper and when I would fight with my siblings, our quarrels would escalate from a threatening word, a whack of the hand, to a hanger, then if the vacuum cords as weapons didn't work, little Hollie grabbing soup cans to throw. (*And that's no joke, though my siblings still like to laugh at me about it.*)

Even our darkest moments offer humor after the healing has had a chance to be cultivated and though we are very close now, most of my childhood memories are rippled with contention.

As the third child, the "runt" of the children at the time, I desired to be respected and violence was my vehicle to gain it. Seeking out respect stemmed from my yearning for freedom and adoration. Attempting to gain what I thought would come through control rather than charisma and kindness.

As years went by, I was actually too shy to speak up for what I really wanted. In groups, I was always the quiet shy girl on the corner that studied everybody else and wished I was were more like them and less like myself.

Once I realized I was just shy and couldn't change it, I began to think less of myself. Not knowing that shyness is not a character trait but a fear, I witheld myself from others as I was too afraid of how others may reject me.

Now, this is not a pity party, or a tale of victimhood as we could probably insert any of our stories here and find just as much of a struggle growing up. I merely share parts of my life stories as an illustration, a parable if you will, so we can all be reminded of how this love associated with our self identity can alter our life choices.

Like many of our own stories and realities, occasionally on our journey we are required to settle. Often we are required to be patient because that is where our life journey is and it doesn't mean that we give up on our dreams or it has to be that way forever. Nor does it mean that we are settling out of a lack of self-love.

This book is an offering of perspective. Self-love can look like a lot of things, even permission to feed our egos, acquire more than we can handle, and burn bridges with selfishness while feeling inferior to the person we truly desire to be.

Together, we can look at ourselves and the excuses we have been using to not expand and be the best version of who we are. To see what it looks like to be the illustrators of how our life should or shouldn't look like, rather than succumbing to another's view of beauty and being.

Settle Up

To settle for less than we deserve would be the ultimate self-imprisonment. Yet, we settle all the time.

In my youth, I felt I was never the best anything. Though I had good grades, they were not the *best*. I had a cute outfit, but it was not the *best* (and I only had <u>one</u>). I had a bike, but it was a girl bike, unlike the boys in the neighborhood with their BMX bikes.

My home was nice, but not the as good as others. I sang in choir but when I got a solo, I completely choked and could not hit my notes because I was too scared to stand up in front of people with their judging ears. When I would have a crush on a boy he was never the cutest because I didn't want to aim too high and be humiliated.

Later in life I found myself going straight into abusive relationships that taught me the exact same principles I learned in childhood; To settle for something and not choose the best. Even entering my marriage at age eighteen with a three-year-old daughter, I knew I wasn't marrying the best choice in a mate, but I was marrying the best I could get, considering my "baggage". I had many mistakes I felt I deserved to be punished for, or at least settle because I created a life that would never be all I was told it should be.

Needless to say I did have a low self-worth. I was used to settling as I figured it's all I deserved. Years of living a dissatisfied life, patiently waiting for it to be better eventually can break us or cause us to seek out a way to fill the starving sensation for a sense of value. Aside from obsessively attempting to create a better self, for better results, we can also flip the coin and become selfish. We get tired of the aching emotional hunger pains and insist on finally getting our turn to be fed.

We begin to feel resentment, entitled and shortchanged by life's blessings.

A defeating the sense of a demanding is often the culprit. Demanding that we receive *all* great things, *all* the time. We want everything because we deserve it, and we get everything wonderful right now because if we *loved* ourselves enough, we would know that we deserve the best always and never settle.

With our demanding mindset, we create a sense of entitlement within us. A sense of being better than someone else. It comes subtly and gradually, even in the form of someone not being "lower" than us, but that we have ascended higher by our efforts.

The ego just loves to thrive on deserving better, especially when it can be attributed to being "earned" by our own efforts and not naturally given gifts. And the world feeds into it by saying, "If you love yourself, you *would* know that you deserve only the best." We forget that *everyone* deserves their desires. Everyone gets the best.

Therefore, when we do have to settle due to the natural process of things, (*even if only temporarily*) we end up feeling like we must not love ourselves because we are settling for less than the best.

When we accept that we do not love ourselves enough, and subsequently *we* are not enough, it becomes easy to dive into self-help addictions, creating self destruction under the guise of self-improvement.

We scrutinize ourselves, we try to fix our flaws into perfection attempting to justify our settling for less. This belief, that if we *better* ourselves we will get to have *better* things, *better* experiences, *better* people in our lives, *better* relationships, etc. Though, there is some truth to who we are and what we attract into our lives, tearing ourselves down to do it never gives us any better results that what we had before. In fact, it creates the opposite by lowering our self worth and settling more often.

We come to these deserve level conclusions and can even grow judgmental, all in the name of self-love. As we rise above our circumstances, our ego can come in to play once again, and we can feel like we deserve the best. Now.

As we notice others settling for less we may become irritated or offer unsolicited advice as we can sometimes still feel the sting of our own past pains from selling ourselves short for so long.

In our crusade to fix ourselves enough to no longer have to tolerate less, we attempt to fix those around us as well. We claim they are just negative thinking or don't know their worth so we tell them, "Hey, you need to love yourself more! Don't settle. Be more." *(Which in reality creates more self doubt now that they have to be told they are not loving enough, and once again, not enough to get what they want).*

None of us wants to be told what another person feels is wrong with us, especially if we never even asked for advice in the first place. "Love yourself more" is no longer the easy answer, it can actually be more destructive than constructive.

This conclusion of why we sometimes settle created in myself the desire to dive into self love deeper and as a result, came this book.

After the thirteen year marriage I had settled for not only ended, but burnt up in a blaze of self doubt, I was left with little self love. Not only was there lies and infidelity that would crush any person's self concept, it was the devastating words that created the most confusion.

My worst nightmare was unfolding into a harsh reality. When we believe we are what others tell us we are, words spoken by a man we love and create a family with as he is leaving have to had some truth to them, right?

"You're no fun, you should be more like your friend's wife."

"I really like big fake boobs."

"You are too into philosophical conversations."

"Your healing work is bullshit."

"You are strong, Hollie, so you can handle this."

I asked for it. I asked for what I could change so I would be worthy of love and to keep my family together. I begged. I promised to change me. Offered a trial period. He even complimented me by saying I was strong, I could handle the putting the pieces of my children's and my lives together. The reality is that I fell completely apart.

These are those darkest of moments when our lives as we know them pass away and a new one must rise from the ashes. The moments that define us, that give us a pathway to create light once again.

I had *thought* I loved myself and was extremely content with my life. I truly felt love on a regular basis. Not because I received it from another person, but because I felt a bursting of love within myself so fully that it felt as if love spilled over onto everyone in my life. I felt the love spill over when hard at work. I felt love in abundance with my friends and family. I didn't notice the areas where love lacked, for I was completely happy. I was obliviously happy for years and I attributed it to the fact that I simply loved myself.

It was during moments of despair, when many "encouraging friends" would tell me I must not love myself, because a woman who loved herself would never beg her husband to stay, would never recommend that he keeps a mistress to keep her marriage.

A woman that loved herself would never still want a husband that would say such horrible things about how he didn't love her anymore.

She would never beg him day after day after day to come back, write letters to him over and over, about how sorry she was that she didn't know he was so unhappy and that she didn't do more or change herself to be what he wanted.

Convinced that I lacked self-love, I sought out to obtain more of this elusive feeling I had heard others profess to possess.

I wanted to feel loved, to feel okay with me and my life as it was. Especially because of the shame I felt for spending many years desiring so much more and being okay with less.

Determined to discover true unconditional love, I jumped into a sea of self-help, diving in and analyzing everything I didn't love about me to create someone more *loveable*. I resolved that if I found all of my flaws, I could either fix them or let go of them and there would be nothing left to not love.

I obsessed. In the past, I would dive into being more spiritually righteous, following checklists as if grading my love deserve level and my right to happiness through my obedience.

Once I was aware of my challenges with love, I struggled to even see that I could make myself any better *(better than all the other sinners of the world at least.)* I felt as if my actions were irrelevant to the love God has for me. I danced the dance but regardless of how I tried to believe that I would be better if I followed all the rules faithfully, my heart would not agree.

I could not seem to gain the comfort or confidence in the world of religion as I once had, so I broadened my areas of study. Open to new ways of thinking and desperate to know what to fix, I became extremely focused on spiritual connection. I felt I was meditating consistently, listened to uplifting music, read every spiritual, relationship, health and parenting book I could possibly find.

I was trying to *self-help* myself to death.

I became so obsessed with fixing whatever it was that was so broken that would've caused a man to not choose me, that I didn't realize there really was nothing to fix. Period. Except of course for my perception of myself.

Enough Love

I was living in the perfect setup for outsiders to remind me of my need of more self-love. I felt frustrated. How could self-love be the answer when I really did feel I loved myself. How do we measure when we love ourselves enough? Is it ever enough?

My business, my passion, my life purpose, for the past eight years was to help people clear their crap so they could love of themselves more. So they could feel like they are enough. To support others in expanding their thinking of deserve level and to allow themselves to have the glorious things of this world and beautiful gifts of the spirit and find better relationships.

When challenged with the idea that I didn't love myself enough I had to really look at some red flags in my own life.

The rebel in me was determined to discover the answer to what I had been blindly accepting as a reason for a hard life. This self-love obsession had come with its rewards. I learned how to fall in love with myself while trying to find everything wrong with me.

I would take myself on solo dates, I would court myself and I learned all kinds of new skills and hobbies. Painting got out emotions and belly dancing allowed me to fall in love with all the jiggly parts of my body! I found adventures like rock climbing, drum making, and frolicking in the woods half naked! I found new experiences and talents I didn't even know were in me. I had gotten to know and love myself so much that I was ready to marry myself.

I became a master at self-love.

It wasn't that I was perfect by any means, or was able to fix any of the flaws. I simply had scrutinized what I could change or distracted myself with new wonderful parts of me so much so, that I had lost the desire to change the flaws. The partnership I had created with myself was an epic one and I loved every minute of it. The more I expanded, the more I was okay with the dim parts of humanity.

Yes, humanity can be dim and it's a good thing. We spend so much time uplifting our spirit and becoming these epic spiritual beings that when we go back to the actual human world it's really dim and very hard to exist in. Think about when we have an amazing church meeting, yoga session, hike or meditation and we are so very uplifted and we feel inspired. We fill hole within ourselves and feel as though we may burst with light and life!

We feel so full of life that we just want to go squeeze somebody and tell them how much we adore them or simply say nothing and gaze into the eyes of another and an honor their soul and honor all of the glorious things we have in the world! Or we feel so connected with nature that we can't wait to lay under the trees and enjoy the serenity of the sweet smelling roses.

We feel as though our whole soul is floating above the earth and nothing can go wrong and everything is beautiful in this perfect world...

....And then as we stub our damn baby toe!!!

We may scream a few curse words that make our children's ears cringe and they drop their jaws in shock. Suddenly, we are once again we are reminded of our humanity and aware of our mortality. The fact that we are human can be really disappointing when were on a spiritual high. And this is where often the disconnect happens between loving ourselves and being okay with the messy human side.

Of course when we're in a spiritual mood, we are completely full of "self-love" because we are simply full of *love*. Prior to the agonizing assault from our furniture to our smallest extremity, we were full of so much hope and light and inspiration that we can't help but feel optimistic about life. And then comes that darn humanity, now we have the chose to feel a plethora of emotions, not just the fuzzy happy ones.

This is where the world comes in and blames the disconnect on our lack of self-love. In our highest spiritual state, would've never settled for the things we settled for as a messy human.

Being human is a delicious experience we get to enjoy food and touch, enjoy thrilling adventures like skydiving and swimming in the ocean, and even curling up and cuddling with a child or cute little puppy!

We get to have all of these joys and we also get to have all of the pains that create opposition. This opposition aids us in understanding how beautiful the beautiful moments really are.

There is no bad or good. It's all good. There's good things and then there's lessons that turn into good thing.

If life was good all the time we would probably find a way to make it bad just so that we can have contrast of experience because we would become very bored. If we did everything perfectly what's the point even living?

One of the best parts of all of the experiences we get to enjoy, is the opportunity to share, to collaborate with each other. When we are authentic and allow ourselves to be messy humans, others feel safe to do the same without judgement and that's when the real magic happens. We connect. We realize we aren't alone. We feel okay to be messy. We accept ourselves *and* others with greater ease.

Rather than using the common term of "self-love", let's consider the term "**self acceptance**". Accepting that we are in fact all **human**. Accepting that we are all going to do stupid stuff sometimes. We are all going to lose our temper and we are all going to lose our cool at times, we may even drop some "F bombs".

We are all going to make a poor decision and suffer for it. We are all going to fall short sometimes. We are all going to have weird quirky unique tendencies and mistakes that only few people get to know.
We are all human, let's relish in it.

This is where "self-love "can't hold a candle to self acceptance.

The Birth of Self Acceptance

Self-love paints the picture that we must love *everything* about ourselves. After years of positive self talk, makeup artist training, deep soul searching and meditating, I can honestly say there are things that I do not love about myself. My flaws.

In relationships, I can guarantee there is *something* we do not love about our significant other, our best friend, even our own children! (*If you have kids already you are not surprised one bit by that comment!*)

We are imperfect. Flaws exist. We can try to convince ourselves to love them over and over again or we can accept that the flaws are there and choose to not let them outweigh the beauty that we do love.

I love that I get to take a lesson from my sweet niece. She is eight years old and filled with pure fierceness. Gianessa is the brightest, most magical girl I have ever seen. Everything she does is pure girl power, with a side of diva.

When she was seven, less than two months after a family tragedy, her hair began to fall out in clumps. Twenty one days later, only a few uneven, sparse patches of hair remained. In less than a month, she had lost 90% of her hair.

I cried for her. Of all the girls in the world, I could not understand why she had to be the one to lose her hair. Since the time she first grew hair, she had always twirled it within her small finger tips. It was her security blanket.

At halloween she always opted to dye it bright colors so that it would last for months, and she loved it. She loved hair, often playing with mine as well. Now it was gone. Her parents faced the challenge of explaining why this was so in terms a seven year old could understand. Luckily, her parents are incredible and equipped with big hearts and understanding ears that have been able to rise to the difficult task.

Fearing a hit to her self esteem, I hosted a fundraiser online and thanks to amazing friends with huge hearts, we raised enough money to buy some wigs to match original hair color to minimize the shock. If she had to lose her hair, we were going to give her a chance to own it and even make it fun by getting her a hot pink wig!

As excited as she was to get to have such wonderful wig options and hats with hair pieces attached, and even with the feeling that everyday got to be dress up day, she eventually chose to not use the wigs. She chose to embrace the beauty of baldness fully and enjoy being comfortable.

In the world of a child, wigs simply were not practical. They itched, and didn't quite stay on when running through a playground, dodging and ducking to avoid the grasp of being tagged "it" or withstanding the natural head perspiration underneath the warm sunshine.

It has been an honor to watch my fierce niece teach me what true fierceness is.

As I have often reflected on why such a girl would be dealt with a large challenge to her self-identity, I remember who she is inside. If she senses any sort of a lack of justice and fairness, she is compelled to voice such (*by voice I mean protest with demands and tears if necessary, until equality has been reached.*)

She is one that requires fairness, and loves feminine beautiful things. Soon after learning to walk, she attempted to walk in her mother's heels and now at age eight, can walk in them better than most women! At a shockingly young age, she has reached the maturity of seeing the beauty in being who she is. This child loves being unique and shining. Of all women I have ever met, she seems to have been born into this world knowing she is a queen and expects to be treated as such.

When children unfamiliar with alopecia make negative comments to her baldness, she has the eye roll down and simply explains that she has alopecia, "duh," and that it is as rare as a unicorn, and continues to explain that she is as wonderful as a unicorn in this world.

She has learned to thrive, to be different and enjoys knowing she is uniquely beautiful. She is remembered in a world where it is easy to forget most people we meet.

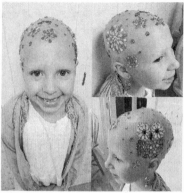

This fierce niece of mine, is the poster child for accepting ourselves as is, even when we don't necessarily like everything about us, seeing that we as a whole are worthy of love and every good thing in the world. This is why my heart chose to donate the proceeds of this ebook sales to the National Alopecia Areata Foundation.

In honor of those that accept themselves and chose to love without condition the beautiful humans they are and hopes to make life a little easier for so many others.

(For more information visit: http://www.naaf.org)

Accepting our flaws takes time, however it is easier without the preconceived notion that unless we *love* every part of ourselves we will not be able to accept that we are perfectly imperfect humans.

When I attended a workshop focused to teach us how to love ourselves more, I was told to stand naked in front of a mirror and as I gaze at my body, to express my love for every part of my body.

I was encouraged tell myself how much I love my stretch marks, as they were reminders of my body once holding my precious child inside me. That my stretch mark "tiger stripes" are badges of honor to be celebrated. At the time I struggled with this concept as I did not like the idea of celebrating my *damaged* body.

As I attempted the exercise however, I realized that I DO love my warrior stripes! Not because they were marks of bravery, but because they were marks of the purest beauty, the beauty of motherhood.

The flaws of my body, my spider veins, stretch marks and saggy boobs, serve as reminders of the beautiful memories I am blessed to hold (*even now that it's been twenty years since my first child was born*). My body, my vessel, expanded and adjusted to nurture the most precious and epic part of my life. I carry my memories with me as I carry love for my children in my heart, even when they are grown and gone, I still get to have my physical souvenirs of the magic of human creation!

I may not love the little lines over my thighs all these years later, but I still get to and smile and feel thankful that I have my flawed legs.

This is true self acceptance verses the self-love lie. I don't have to love the actual appearance of my "old-lady-wrinkle-faced" backside to love the feeling it gives me when I notice it.

Though beholders of what I consider my beautiful body may not always agree to its beauty, my love and acceptance of myself is the most powerful opinion that actually matters.

Confidence is simply shared self-acceptance.

When we accept all of the pieces of ourselves, we expect the same from others and we are more accepting of others. It is the perfect recipe for cultivating authentic and loving connections.

With our continued self acceptance, we create more dynamics to in our relationships around us. Real conversations occurring allows weaknesses to show. Though we have been trained to hide most weakness, and to avoid drawing attention to flaws, sometimes to share them allows us to gain support and can be mutually beneficial.

I love to write. Writing is my passion, my process and my joy. Math is not. During remodels of my home I have come to learn just how much I use math and am capable, but also how much longer it takes me. As I want to learn and do more, I have found there are many new friends in my life great at both math and construction.

By being vulnerable enough, I have been blessed with new people to join my life. Not only does this create beautiful bonds, it allows me to receive support and generous assistance when needed! What a beautiful way to live in a community!

Think of all the times we missed out on something by not being brave enough to show our flaws and allow support to flow to us. It's okay to not have everything figured out, to be stumped sometimes. That's what creates the best friendships *and* stories!

Loving YOUR version of you!

We start out as a blank slate in life. Loved and adored, sometimes before we are even born in this world. We are loved even when we are merely a thought of one day existing in our parent's minds. As we move through life and into adulthood, it can be difficult to drop all the ideals of love that we were given throughout our youth. Like a sponge we soaked in everything that we were told. The praise we received allowed us to soak up what is good. The scolding and punishments we received taught us what was bad.

We grew into complex adults filled with standards of worth, acceptable appearances and behaviors and the expectations of what our adulthood *should* look like.

The programming we receive as we mature is wonderful for teaching us how to avoid pitfalls.

For example,

in Africa, it's important to know how to not get eaten by a lion.

Russia, how not to freeze to death.

In the congo, how to avoid giant mosquitos.

The self preservation programming is not a bad thing, this is part the reason we have families. Parents and communities teach us and keep the progression and advancement of our species moving forward in evolution. It seems however in modern times that this way of guidance has in some ways grown detrimental to much of our ability to improve when the influence continues into our adult lives.

Unrealistic expectations, pressure to perform, rigorous scrutiny to gain perfection can lead many of us to escape through substance abuse, addictions and ambivalence. When the bar is set so high it is near impossible to reach, we feel defeated before we begin and often won't even try.

When it is too low and we receive praise for little or no effort, we feel we deserve more reward for less work and a sense of entitlement comes into play.

Both of these scenarios create the perfect storm for a life of seeking the forever unobtainable "self-love" and the golden goose excuse why everything hasn't worked out the way we want it to.

When we have accomplished a plethora of successes, we can still feel a lack of accomplishment. Despite our progress and achievements, we may feel as if it wasn't enough. That *we* are not enough. This is because the list of accomplishments came not from within ourselves, but from outside influences such as society, media and our own families.

Regardless of how close we get to hitting the bar of expectations, we feel we fail even when we skim the bar with our fingertips verses grasping hold of the impossible standards.

In the "all or nothing" world of success, we end up feeling defeated. We resolve to do more, assess more and fix more to reach higher next time.

Contrastingly, when we always succeed because our expectations are so low to the ground, we feel a lack of a sense of purpose or satisfaction within ourselves. We meet the expectation and mediocre validation effortlessly. Since we feel within we are capable of more, it becomes discouraging, draining and limits our desire to ever reach for anything more.

A common part of this struggle with the sense of failure and dissatisfaction, is that it does not dissolve by claiming "self-love". We can not adore and praise ourselves if the level by which to gauge our actions, or whether we as a being are worthy of love was not *created* by us and was the creation of another's standards.

Help Yourself

We claim self-love to be an inside job, yet let external influence determine not only if we are lovable and worthy to love ourselves, but also the amount of acceptance we feel for ourselves based on our actions.

Wading through the pool of expectations can be a lengthy process when it feels like an obligation to avoid more pain. Self scrutiny can be a hard habit to break.

I love to read, I love the stories of others and the inspiration that comes through hearing the powerful journeys taken through the trenches of adversity. Influences for improvement await my ready fingertips at all times to support any

43

motivations for improvement or growth. In any given room in my home, you will find self-help books, inspirational card decks and journals. I don't dive into all of them all the time but I do insure they are easily available *(similar to setting a big bowl of fruit out and watching kids choose fruit first when snack cravings hit)*. If it's easy to see and grasp, we are more likely to utilize it.

Although improvements are healthy and keep us from stagnancy, improving can become detrimental. There was once a time in my life I once dubbed myself a "self help junkie". The gap between where I was and all that I wanted to be, seemed simply too overwhelming. I resolved that if I *fixed* more of myself, I would be able to achieve my dreams faster.

At any given time, a collection of self-help books teaching different concepts from religion to business, decorating with feng shui to cooking healthy foods, and from people skills to parenting. I would study at the first light of the sunrise before my day started and listen to audio recordings in the car in place of the loud music I previously enjoyed.

I would enjoy a book when on the elliptical or stationary bike at the gym to pass the boredom of exercise and allow me to feel my time was worthwhile. At bedtime I would cozy up in a pile of blankets, warm tea and what I felt was my most needed self-improvement read of the day, with journal in hand taking detailed notes.

My study of self improvement continued for years. I loved knowing I was improving myself, that I would be better because of the knowledge and application of what I focused on. What I had not realized, was how my obsession with bettering myself was in fact, destroying me.

It *felt* as though I was feeding my brain, soaking up the wealth of wisdom from the discovered secrets of the experts. At night I would lay my head on my pillow exhausted but with a mind filled with all that I was going to do better the next day. And that wonderful mind of mine would churn and churn and churn through what I had taken in for the day.

My brain would analyze new outcomes and scenarios of how to react differently, take action differently and how it would look to have my life actually be different. This was the perfect formula for a slumber that is anything *but* restful. By morning I would feel a new sense of urgency to improve, knowing how much was still lacking from what I studied the day prior, and once again repeat the cycle of pouring in the positive study to create positive change. I was completely oblivious to the negative effects of all the positive influences.

What I had not realized in my world of improvement, was the demolition occurring underneath the surface of the conscious actions I was taking. Each moment of each day, I was telling myself that I was not enough. That what I had to offer everyone and everything in my life needed massive improvement to be deemed as "good". Restless energy turned into obsession and perfectionism. To control myself was to control my world, even down to what I would or would not allow myself to feel.

Though blinded to the destruction of any self worth of my gifts, or love for myself, I managed to be quite successfully in many areas and feel happiness. I felt happiness because I *told* myself I was happy.

I constantly reminded myself that I was happy through affirmations, through living a life that in my preconceived mental image of what happiness looked like, I had all that was needed to have it. I resolved that I had a good life and was going to be successful in any endeavor I chose. Of course it would eventually be true, for how could I study so much and not make progress? I was convinced that the sewing of seeds into my garden of potential would yield perfect fruit, unlike the small potatoes I'd been churning up.

In order to believe the greatest of lies we tell ourselves, the lies must have threads, even ropes of truth woven through them. By seeing the truth in our lies, we can easily stop seeing anything that contradicts what we already know to be true.

If there were no truth, there would be no lies, not just because everything has it's perfect opposite, but because the farther fetched a lie is, the less likelihood anyone will believe it, especially if its a lie we have authored. Grasping to the smallest shred of truth makes all the lies we tell ourselves actually believable.

One of the great lies that ruled my life and made it easy for me to use the self-love excuse, is the lie of perfectionism.

The belief that we are here to become perfect. *(Meaning the older we get, the more we should have our shit together, figured life out and progressed to be able to competently improve.)* We should be getting better with age, even though the reality is that as we age, we discover new challenges and new ways to be a messy human, piss people off and feel more emotions.

Being loved more and having what we create loved more does not change based on how perfect we are. It doesn't even change by loving ourselves more. In fact, having more love for the results of what we create, especially in the name of loving ourselves more, only creates a deeper sense of perfectionism.

Perfectionism is the catalyst for improvement and the destruction of acceptance.

Perfectionism kills the creation of possibilities. When we attempt to align our world in within a box of expectation, we stop thinking of what we can create outside the box and scrutinize what is in the box. We may have the most exact right angles in every corner, immaculate walls worthy of praise and even frame our success on the wall so perfectly, any level would be put to a crooked shame. However wonderful the validation feels to have succeeded and cultivated such high expectations into existence, we are also creating pure distraction from what *could* have been created given freedom to create with the same resources.

We can use our creative imagination to figure out how to create what has already been done by others and is expected by others, or we can use that same natural tool to create something as exciting and unique as we are!

The hardest step is always letting go of what we thought would be and allow ourselves to imaging what could be. Most of us only figure out how to let go of past imaginations and expectations when they are taken from us. It's easy to choose a new path when one has been destroyed in front of you. To choose the higher road when the lower road is ripped from your grasp. We all have an experience of some sort of loss, of a divergent of our path.

Soon after having my second child, postpartum hit me pretty hard. In a tiresome struggle to feel of value, I remember spending days upon days steaming my kitchen tile floors, scrubbing the grout with a toothbrush and bleach as to have an immaculate home. At the end of the day, my achy sore low back was proof that I was a good mother and a great wife. It was tangible proof that I was contributing something to my family. A visual "pat on the back", I needed to feel okay with the world around me.

I wore my cleanliness badge of honor with pride, knowing there was not a single person that could claim to have floors as clean as mine. Perfection was the ultimate goal.

Perfectionism thrives on validation. The less we get from others the more we can scrutinize over insignificant things. Often we throw around the excuse of, *"I'm just a perfectionist"* and call it a reason to be critical, scrutinize, controlling or just plain anal about the way things are done. We attribute our perfection claims to our personality type and that meticulousness is required to be associated with us.

For many of us the temptation of *control* in the world around us is simply too great to resist. We even become stellar at influencing others to do things OUR way verses THEIR way, increasing our sense of *correctness.* Talk about power and control! Whether a clean house, party planning, parenting, business processes or even cooking, we thrive on being the wise authority. At the end of the day not only do we get a control high, we feel an enormous amount of validation by how well things were done, the *right* way. *Our way.*

There is a point in life when most of us resolve to no longer value the outside opinions of others, to no longer need to be *right*.

Though very different for many of us, they all give us empowerment over our own world. For instance, I can choose to discredit options outside my religious views, outside my family, outside my educational class. I can pick and choose the advice I will receive or won't receive. I am the God of my thoughts. (*At least until a super villain successfully creates a mind-control ray and takes over the world.*)

We filter what we hear all the time, however we filter it with prejudice on what is or isn't acceptable. With such an insatiable power, such pure control, such greatness, isn't it odd that the majority of the time we give that very power up to those that are not in any position to be offering us advice? As soon as we let go, we gain true power over ourselves and the need to feel "***in power***" vs. "***empowered***".

When I would teach makeup application, one of my favorite phrases to remind women to pay attention of what advice they were receiving was,

"Never go to a dentist that doesn't have any teeth!"

Why would we allow someone to advise us on proper dental hygiene if what they were doing to their own mouth was not the results we wanted? Yet we allow ourselves to be influenced and powerless against the views, opinions and standards of others.

We allow a child's comment about our jiggly thighs or a stranger's disapproving sigh dictate whether or not we are adequate in our actions and presentation of ourselves into society. We feel a loss of our own power and therefore create situations to feel a sense of control again, in power once again. These perfectionist tendencies only put power in the external world around us, they are in fact not giving *us* any real power. We are at the mercy of every outer influence and starving our personal empowerment in the process.

In case this concept has not yet crossed your mind, I am about to reveal a hard truth. One that may seem harsh, or hilarious to you even though it is quite true.

No matter how wonderful you are, how successful, attractive, or kind you show up as, no matter how much you have or give, NOT EVERYONE WILL LIKE YOU.

The best business advice I have ever received was by my business coach, Angella Johnson of Soul Vision Business, years ago as I was just launching my first LLC. After spending a lengthy amount of time healing some very heavy, very difficult emotional trauma with a client, I received a complaint about my service offerings and the cost via a very lengthy email.

I called my business coach at the time to confide in her and to admit what I was certain was a complete business failure. This client had met with me, hugged me, we cried, we cleared emotional crap, she said it changed her life for the better, and yet, this client came back rejecting my heart's passion, my life purpose.

I sobbed to my sweet coach. I could not fathom someone rejecting what I felt was inspired by angels.

53

(Because if it were of angels, and they are enlightened how could anything be wrong enough to be rejected?)

Do you see the rabbit hole we can dive deep into within our minds?

Do you see the power stripped right from my own thoughts?

Do you hear the slap across the face to, "Pull it together woman!" sweet Angella must have wanted to offer me?

Her response was perfect and I can to this day hear the smile in her voice as she said, "Well Hollie, congratulations!"

"Congratulations?!" I repeated back shockingly as it was hardly the response I expected.

"Yes! Congratulations! This means you are on the right track. All things good in this world experience resistance. Every successful person has up to 10% of people that don't support them. There will always be those that oppose what you create, regardless of how inspired it may be. So congrats! You have made it!"

I was stunned. I wanted to quit right there.

The depths I hurt from just one rejection made me not want to ever have another. What if I get *loads* of rejections? What if people publicly call me out and say I am wrong? What if people hate what I create? Or think I'm stupid? Or egotistical? What do I know about anything anyway?

Often when we are hit with the truth, our excuses can win the battle between our minds and hearts and it can take some time to soak in. I took her advise the best I could and resolved to allow myself to agree with her. I was now a "professional" because someone wasn't happy 100%.

Then I cried for a week.

A week y'all! Seven full days of avoiding talking to people, *(unless to vent about the client that didn't like me and get validation of how likable I am of course.)* A week withholding advice out of fear it would not be received well. I allowed myself to doubt the miracles I had seen due to the opinion of **one** person.

I didn't want to take on any new clients and postponed scheduling anything that wasn't already on the books. In my world the current clients were "safe" as I knew without a doubt they loved what I offered them. How could I risk anyone new? How could I risk what I was told was inevitable rejection?

Then it happened. A new client was referred to me. A choked up voice message recording, *(which no doubt left a soggy tear drenched phone on the other end.)* a sweet soul asking for help. A stranger, a person that mattered simply because they existed and a choice to be made from someone that was just fuming about *one* person's angry email.

The ego that shielded me from future embarrassments and pains, went right out the window. I figured if she hated me, she was already an obvious emotional mess so I couldn't do much worse. I chose to pack up my pity party, forget about me and simple give because I was asked to. Ultimately, I wanted to, and this was my excuse to not be perfect.

Like all fears we have in our heads, I haven't had near the devastation I thought I would. The simple voice in my head from a brilliant coach and friend, "10% won't like what you have to offer the world." reminds me that I'm not better than anyone else. I am not immune to being human, others are not immune to mixing my messages or misinterpreting my intentions.

Here's that harsh truth again, not everyone will like us or what we do. By becoming **better**, you do not change that cold, hard, fact of life.

We can however, change whether or not,

- We allow other opinions to matters to us.

- We allow outside views to take us away from better things by distracting or stopping us.

- We allow external standards make us doubt our abilities.

Yes, we can have our power taken away. Influences and opinions of others can affect us like a jagged piece of kryptonite has been lodged into our brain stopping us from our ability to choose our thoughts and views of ourselves. We feel powerless, so we once again seek to be *in power verses empowered.*

We are influenced by the outside, therefore we seek to control the outside world. From the time we are born, we are programmed to believe what we are told about ourselves. Our entire existence was dependent upon whether or not our parents felt the desire to feed and protect us.

If we were not worth loving enough to be taken care of, how could we survive? We were groomed into the people we are today by others views and opinions. We will continue to be groomed and influenced until we choose to do our own internal influencing.

Break the List

We know we are falling subject to perfectionism, self doubt and a lack of self acceptance when we create our self improvement list. The less we can accept of ourselves the more we desire to fix what remains unacceptable.

To be buried in the cemetery alongside the "self-love" excuse, is the **Fix It List.** or as I like to rename it the **Break Me List.** While in the guise of a *Fix It List,* we parade around listing all the attributes we dislike, the bad habits, the times we lost our patience and our temper, the times we didn't measure up to the expectations of others or the comparisons we created within ourselves.

When we mask our feelings of inferiority with a resolve to "change for the better" rather than realizing we already *are* better if we would just quit with the damn lists!

Don't get me wrong, I love lists. To-do lists that keep my brain free from churning useless information or keep me from forgetting a sack lunch for my kids on field trip day or to pay the utility bill to keep my water on. Lists have a wonderful purpose, however, we are not one of them.

Lists are for things, not people.

To list what we will "fix" about ourselves, is to list what we do not like and have deemed unacceptable for our existence on this planet. Once again, this is under the illusion that if we were to be better we would be loved more, even if only by ourselves. The problem with the list of items to fix within ourselves, is that all it really does is break us. It takes away the humanity, the quirkiness, the flaws and only leaves inputs and outputs. Buttons. Tasks. Consequential love.

Similar to making a grocery list of all that is needed for the upcoming week for meals then going to the fridge expecting to see an abundance of food. The fridge will look empty every time as the lack has been our focus. We can miss the fact that half the meal items may be sitting on the shelves, we only see what there is to add in order to correct the void.

When it comes to falling in love, we often *list* reasons why we love someone. Then one day BOOM! Tragedy strikes and stroke hits. Do we still love that person even if they can't play the guitar like they once did? Kiss us every so sweetly and softly? Why would we love someone that doesn't have the original hundred reasons we fell in love with them?

Because we love people, not things. We list things, not people.

Conditional love says, "I love you because of this list of reasons of how you make me happy or bring me joy."

Unconditional love says, "I love you. Just because I love you."

We know what unconditional love is when we love children. They can be the biggest brats at times, throw a full-on tantrum in the middle of the most breakable section of the most expensive counter in the store. You would never hear a mother say,

"I love my little two year old Timmy because he is so enthusiastic with his loud screams and falling arms. I just love the thrill I get when my adrenaline soars not knowing if he will throw his foot long, ironman toy through a glass perfume case."

In fact, most moms act on full restraint to avoid screaming back at the tempered two year old!

Timmy is a child that only knows what he wants and has not learned empathy or awareness outside his own little body. He only knows to take what he needs to feel good *(as he should, his is a toddler)*. Timmy's mom loves him because he simply exists. Two year old fits, spits, fists and all, she loves him, unconditionally.

Think of who are considered the most unlovable people of the world, folks on death row that have committed the most heinous of crimes. They still have visitors, people that actually still love them, unconditionally.

You are probably not a murderer on death row, and you have learned that earth shattering tantrums in stores are not a desirable way to get what you want, so it's safe to say it's easy to love you unconditionally too. So there is no need for you to have a "break it" list requiring you to change all the flaws in order to receive acceptance.

Self-Less-Ness

As we reflect on our relationship with ourselves and our relationship with others and how they view us viewing ourselves, it can be a lot to sort out. If we were to view much of what we are taught by society and religion, to think of ourselves can be considered selfish.

One such view is that we are to be the bottom of the totem pole in the hierarchy of needs. We are to put others first if we are to be truly humble, loving and contributing to the world in a godly sense. It is only when we are acting as the dust from which we are created, that we are able to be accepted and loved. Though our desires are from a place of love, it seems that all too often this has the opposite effect.

What do we do with dirt? We STEP on it. We walk all over it. When it comes into our homes we

DESPISE it and do all we can to remove it from our lives! Yes, we love dirt when it is where we want it to be, with our plants and outside like we love wild animals but don't get too close to them either.

In the name of wanting to be loved by God and others, we make ourselves less important. We strive to be "SELFLESS" or less than we are. Less worry from others, less time for us, less needing attention from others. The more lonely, ignored and forgotten we feel the more we cleave to validation from not only our creator, but any humans that will recognize how lowly we are.

Recently, I lost a mother. The most common remarks whispered at her funeral were,

"She gave so much to so many."
"She never thought of herself."
"Her hobby was service."

...And my heart would sink.

I was twelve years old when this woman joined our family taking on a new life, moving to a new state and adding five step-children to her family of two young girls. Over the next twenty years she gave. She gave and gave and gave. She was the type of grandma to my children that would drive three hours just to watch my son strikeout in his baseball game, in the rain, smiling the whole time just to return home late and wake in the dark hours of the morning to go deliver mail.

I do admire her love and desire to help. I do miss her dearly. I was not able to be there for her passing as it was a sudden failing of the heart and was completely unexpected. Of course it had to be her heart.

I stood alone next to the body she left behind, applying makeup ever so carefully and desperately wanting her beauty to show even in death. As I believe the body reflects our emotional state through specific ailments, my thoughts centered around her sweet tender heart. I had but one question to ask her *(as I always do when someone I love passes)*.

"Were you loved *enough*?" I whispered, caressing her hand so light yet fervent. I wanted to know if she regretted *always* giving. Always being last on the list. I had felt regret not showing her more love, doing more for *her.* The answer was felt and

66

heard in my mind more than an audible answer, but a clear answer just the same.

The answer came as a strong yet soft affirmative. I felt reminded that there are many places and ways to feel love even if one or two areas may have fallen short. It would seem she had accepted things as they were and all of her expectations for love had been met.

One of the interesting parts about being selfless, is it seldom occurs to others receiving how little is actually given to someone that *always* gives all. It becomes a way of life. Even with the desire to give, the attempt to give, it is most often declined and eventually, forgotten. If we offer a cookie to someone everyday, and every day we are told, "No thanks." Eventually, we will stop offering and assume they are happy in their cookie-less world, as is and may even feel shame for continuing to offer the cookie option.

When we hold too tightly to the idea of achieving selflessness, we stop ourselves from receiving what we need. We become accustomed to feeling validation for what we give and do to the point that we lose all sight of being loved and accepted just for simply existing. We are following the belief that love is based on our works, not on our soul. While it is true that the works *reflects* the soul, the heart, and our character, it is our works and actions that are simply what we do *with* what we are; not, who we are or why we receive love.

Love exists for us, because we exist.

Think of our babies. A baby starts life as a parasite in the womb. Robbing our mother's body of nutrients if she does not take in enough surplus for herself. Once we are born, we require constant attention, energy and time. We take food and give only smelly messes and sleepless nights in return. Yet, from the time of conception, we are loved. Even as those terrible two's mentioned earlier creep in, we are loved. As is.

As a messy human, we are cherished, celebrated and adored. Yet at some point, we can learn that we are not enough. We learn that we must earn our place in this world. We can believe that others deserve more than we do. We can choose to site childhood, traumas, misunderstandings, society, the media, etc. for this conditioning, yet often a simple acceptance of what is all that is required to create change.

Once we begin to understand that by simply existing, we deserve love just as much as a small child that doesn't know any better, and if we accept that we are loved regardless of what we do, we get to allow ourselves to do because we *love* doing, not because others love us for doing. We give because we love giving, not the validation we feel from doing so.

Selfishness

The pendulum always swings both ways. There is always an opposite. As such, the extreme opposite to selflessness is selfishness.

Just as we can cleave to the belief that we don't deserve as much as others, there is a belief that forms that we deserve *more* than others. Convinced that the world needs to set an imaginary deficit right. The harsh truth is that we have all been wronged in some way at some point. The difference is the view that life must be fair and we somehow have suffered more than others. Selfishness is a tricky belief to break as we become masters of justification.

I will be the first to admit that I have been selfish at times, we all have because we are human *(just in case you forgot today)*. Most often a sign that we are being selfish is unveiled the same manner that those old friends the black pot and kettle teach us, we can see the flaws in others easiest when we hold them within ourselves.

Much like self*less*ness, selfishness is a sign of a deficit. In contrast to an emptiness filled by validation in giving to others, our selfishness creates within us a black hole that never can be filled. A thirst that will never be quenched. If we are always thirsting for more, how can anything ever be enough? Especially if an offering of time, love, material things would leave us always remaining in a state that lacks ever feeling satiated.

When what is given is never enough, it is easy to look around and assume the deficit is in the people and situations around us, not within ourselves. Our eyes rest on the top outermost part of our bodies, not deep down in the soul.

We will continue seeking to soothe the deficit, to fill the hole inside.

71

We can try and fix it ourselves by demanding perfectionism, or being treated and loved *our* way (*as we always know best*). We also relish in love, attention and adoration, feeling we earn all that is given and most often reciprocation is long overdue. It becomes easy to fall in love when we feel we are worshiped for our greatness, adored and recognized as being elite.

A deficit like this, is what often is meant when we give the advice of "love yourself more", however the illusion this self love implies looks a lot more like narcissism.

The self-love excuse is a narcissist's free ticket to the "ME -TRAIN".

A narcissist is defined as:
"A person who has an excessive or interest in admiration of themselves."

As trendy as this word is becoming for describing every ex-spouse, asshole or rude person in the checkout line at the grocery store that cut in front of us, it does describe perfectly the extreme "self-love" has taken in a lot of our world today.

Of the many reasons we could speculate how a narcissist comes into creation, one common denominator is a feeling of lack at some point *(a.k.a. the black hole)*. Most narcissists express wanting to be loved, successful or cherished, even when acting like a sociopath. Actions, even hurtful ones, are justified by the black hole of desire never able to be filled by an outside love.

The more we focus on "self-love" and the more we love ourselves, the easier it becomes to get what we want. Always having others easily give the love can create a sense of entitlement and selfishness, leading to narcissism if gone unbridled.

Do we deserve all the best things in life simply because we exist? Of course we do! Do we deserve it at the expense of another? Hell NO!

There is always a way to have all we desire without taking it from another or requiring another to give it to us. This is the difference between egotistical narcissism and true self appreciation. Words are powerful and telling someone to love themselves is an easy way to push them to a "ME-train" of selfishness.

As I mentioned earlier, I do love spending time with myself, giving to myself, even dating myself. I also enjoy spending time with others, giving to others and dating others. Not because of what others give or do for me, but because I love people, love the stories, the views, the laughter.

In contrast, when we have taken self-love to the *extreme* self-love, we love people, because if feels good to have others give and validate to us. Generally, the more selfish we become, the more we surround ourselves with other "givers" versus other "takers".

If we are the type of person to take and require more, relationships with a fellow "taker" won't last long. Generally, a mutual dissatisfaction will end the relationship in the early stages as there isn't much to gain from each other in the beginning.

As givers, we love how wonderful it feels to give, the validation of someone relishing in our offering gives us a reason to exist, a reason for being, a reason to keep putting ourselves below those those that offer validation to us.

We all get to have a little give and take within ourselves. We get to experience moments when we act on narcissistic tendencies acting for our own benefit above all others as well as the givers stance and give more than we receive. It's all about balance and all about accepting that we are both light and dark. Loving and giving most of the time and on occasion an asshole. It's called being a human.

If we procrastinate finding the balance within ourselves, we will naturally find balance with others around us. Anytime we are extreme to one side, in order to create balance there must be an extreme to another side. Unless we keep ourselves in check, we will be gifted the chance to see the contrast by attracting individuals and situations into our lives that will call out the extremes in us.

For awhile the opposition feels refreshing, it pulls us closer to a form of center. Why do you think opposites attract so often?

However, as time continues, the friction of the opposition forms and that's when we either push back out to our extremes or find a way to meet in the middle. If we choose drawing ourselves to the middle ground, and discover we are alone or disappointed with the results, we tend to launch ourselves back out to the furthest extreme once again, now with and added bit of spite and stubbornness under our belt, for it "didn't work before" or was "painful".

Set in our ways, it can be as if we are asking for experience to force us to jump outside of our patterns through either pain or pleasure in hopes of discovering our balance once again.

Because we are human, part of our experience in this life *is* to experience all emotions. How will we learn if we don't move through the positive and the negative actions in our world.

We all get to be selfish at times, selfless in moments and do it over and over and over again until we find the balance that fits our unique journey.

Self-Care-Ness

Although extremes feel intense and allow us to feel alive, they are hardly what we would desire for everyday life. Through self awareness, we can see when we have let ourselves flow to an extreme version and balance back out. Often the extremes of selflessness and selfishness are simply a sign that it's time for some selfcare-ness. *(Yes, I am aware that "self care-ness" is not a word, and I accept that I use fake words at times.)*

Self-care-ness is the state of being in self care mode. It differs from the term self-love as it illustrates action of taking care of ourselves.

Self care is all about what we say to ourselves, do to ourselves, do for ourselves and require others to do for us.

It's about knowing who we are and what we expect and following through while allowing a balance of selflessness and selfishness. It's not the one size fits all, cookie cutter solution to finding that balance of self we seek. Because it requires us to see ourselves on the inside, evaluate who is in there, what we want, what is missing, what or who gets to come into play or who or what gets to leave our lives. Since we may have been operating contrary to this way of being for some time, a guideline can offer a start of new habits and way of thinking.

Self care isn't always just about bubble baths. It's about a state of mind, a state of being. If we only care for ourselves on the surface it will remain superficial. Rather than giving a list of what we do to show self-care-ness, let's look at how to keep our minds focused on self care for the soul.

To care for something that has been left uncared for, always requires some sort of clean up, destruction or disassembling.

An overgrown garden requires old bushes, trees and massive weeding efforts.

A decayed or molded house requires stripping and ripping out the damage.

Chipped and faded paint requires sanding and scraping.

Home foundations require leveling the ground on site.

Even a meal preparation requires trimming of fat, peeling, cutting.

So often we fear the destructive states, forgetting that it is required for constructing.

If we choose to not remove the decay, the decay will fester and spread to what we create. If we choose to avoid a little destruction before rebuilding, all will eventually be destroyed and the change, (whether to rebuild or let go) will be *forced* upon us.

It is when we embrace the change, that we are able to actually enjoy the elation that comes from progress through destroying what is no longer bringing joy to our lives.

In preparation for selling our family home, I found great relief in discovering how to use a chainsaw. (*Chainsaws always create great stories, right?!*)

It was a destruction I hadn't ever foreseen as even being a possibility. After eleven years and adding two children to our family, our home was our sanctuary. I spent countless hours inside and outside creating a yard that felt like my own mini forest.

After my husband left, I realized the downside to not having my name on the mortgage. From my view at the time, the choice to stay married was not mine. The choice to sell was not mine. The choice to work outside the home was not mine. Now I was faced with all the work required to increase our resale value in hopes I would get some sort of scraps from the home equity.

My soon-to-be-ex-husband loved sour green Granny Smith apples. Years prior he ate one so delicious he saved the seeds, nurtured them for weeks, grew a sprout, acclimatized it to the outdoors and carefully planted it in the center of our front yard. The front yard that we had planned to be "clean trees" *(meaning no fruit, sap, or seeds to make a mess to clean on the sidewalks or cars).* The backyard was for the fabulous fruit trees, seed trees and all the messy goodness a forest can offer.

The ultimate sin had been committed the year prior, when I had planted an "autumn blaze maple" in the center of back yard. The landscaping was my domain, it was my passion and my pastime. It hadn't occurred to me anyone would object to a fantastic shade tree that offers celebratory red flamed leaves ringing in the fall season. The pictures I saw online were magical to say the least. I had thought it would be the perfect shade tree for the children's sandbox I planned to one day build and offer refuge from the sun for the sensitive part of the vegetable garden.

I supported the green apple tree even when he planted it in front. I figured I could be flexible. I loved the wee little apples, even after discovering it was planted there to spite my breaking the sacred tree rules he and I had agreed to in our suburban paradise.

My justifications didn't matter, I broke the rules and now to make it fair, he did as well.

Over the years, his sour green apple tree grew beautifully. With three trunks, it shot up taller than our house! Taller than any other tree in the yard! It blossomed and bore many, many tiny green sour apples the worms and birds loved, year after year. *(While my glorious, artistic celebration of shade died soon after being planted.)*

As I surveyed my home in preparation to sell, curb appeal and changes needed, I could not look passed what had become an eyesore to me. I love plants, especially the trees, especially *fruit* trees. This tree however, had it coming.

I can only imagine the array of craziness my poor neighbors must've observed as I awkwardly wielded my chainsaw and new found power hidden beneath the branches of the front yard as I took out my rage and lack of control in my life on a defenseless, apple tree grown so carefully.

Friendly, *(or concerned)* passersby offered what must have been witty remarks or encouragement, I had my headphones in so I couldn't hear them. Cars would slow and even stop as neighbors took time out of the hustle and bustle of their daily lives to gauge whether I was in a positive or negative emotional state. But I didn't care. I was busy freeing myself. I was busy *destructing.*

I sliced into one of the three trunks and as the saw created a cloud of apple wood dust in the air, *(like glitter but without the sparkle)* I will admit I felt like a badass. It felt good to destroy. I removed the second trunk. Watching as the towering tree fell to the ground. I felt a thrill of empowerment, *(even while in-power)* and then chopped it up even more to fit in the trash cans. I did leave *one* of the tree trunks, *(I'm not a complete monster)* and what remained was celebrated. I *chose* to leave it. I had control over *something* in my life.

As a gazed at the yard, it looked less overgrown, less messy, more like there was a well thought out plan the whole time. I had created physical clarity and at the same time, gave myself clarity and confidence. This chain saw therapy was a type of destruction that aided me to move through what I was feeling and could not express.

Creating self careness means allowing the destruction needed. Cutting away all that is no longer supporting what we desire most in our lives.

At this part of my life it was years of passive aggressiveness represented by an overgrown tree cut out with a chainsaw.

What we need to cut out of our lives is as unique as we are, it can be an item given to us that holds a memory that isn't pleasant, a sink full of dirty dishes, a home that doesn't serve us in a location that doesn't support us, or even association with beliefs that feel more like going through motions on auto-pilot rather that a true heartfelt belief system.

To destroy is to remove. Destruction only creates a sense of lack if we say it does. We can always rebuild on nothing, but if we rebuild on the same crap we just get the same crap, and it stinks.

Cutting out what doesn't truly support us can also mean people.

If we have never needed to end an unhealthy relationship, we are not living or we are being a dirty doormat. We know it is time to disassemble relationships when people make us feel more tired after being around them, make us feel like we are not good enough yet, or make us feel like we are anything less than absolutely loveable. As is.

84

That thing that's nagging you? Do it or let it go. It's not that important or you would have done it by now. We act our lives out in alignment with our priorities. What is most important to us is naturally displayed in what actually is accomplished in our lives.

Love your Life your way

I hope these insights have created your own inspired thoughts and allowed you to move one step closer to accepting all the parts of you, the lovely parts, the together parts, the silly parts and those damn messy parts too!

My prayer is that some portion of your heart has been inspired to allow a stirring desire of change to create the self acceptance and life enjoyment we all desire.

All my love and belief,
~Hollie Hope

About the Author

Hollie Hope has been assisting others in clearing negative perspectives and emotional blocks for over a decade through intuitive healing and listening to inspiration from angels among us. Her first love is her three children and "fur-babies", though her passion for life stems from being surrounded by the simple beauty of nature and is fueled by sharing the wisdom and life lessons she has gained throughout her journey.

She fulfills her dreams through assisting with the creation of books, retreats, private clearing sessions and an avid hiking buddy among her home in southern Utah.

Hollie is a full supporter of the National Alopecia Areata Foundation in honor of her sweet niece, as she adjusts to her recent hair loss. www.naaf.org.

Another passion she shares is to assist women to discover their worth through a nonprofit organization which includes a mentoring program. Hollie has been honored Women of Worth Utah to be able to volunteer with this organization since 2011.

Visit www.wowutah.org for more information.

Special thank you to the epic people in my life. specifically:

The Talented Photographer, Brittany Hollinshead

Angella Johnson, Soul Vision Business
www.angellajohnson.com

Design & Marketing: Melanie Baxendale
www.wikidmarketing.com

For more information or upcoming events, visit
www.holliehope.co.

"Love Your Beauty"

The
BEAUTY of
PERSPECTIVE

WWW.THEBEAUTYOFPERSPECTIVE.COM

Made in the USA
San Bernardino, CA
02 November 2018